To Stacey—
May you & yo[...]
blessed always — Brenda

Beyond My Rainbow

By
Brenda B. Berggoetz

PublishAmerica
Baltimore

Softcover 9781413763331
PUBLISHED BY PUBLISHAMERICA, LLLP
www.publishamerica.com
Baltimore

Printed in the United States of America

*I dedicate this book to my mother and greatest fan,
Rosemary Berggoetz Arnett,
for all her love and support
and to
my most beautiful children
and grandchildren
for all their blessings*

*I would also like to acknowledge my very special
grandparents
Bridget Loretta Connor Hayes
and
John Joseph Whitehouse Hayes
for all their love,
the many times they read poetry to me,
and for all the poetry my grandmother wrote
but never had published -
Forever in Love*

The Separation

Darkness looms all around
as a neverending forest,
reality is tainted
as my vision becomes obscured.

Heart lies absent
as my mind recedes into numbness,
fatigue abounds through my body
while pain consumes the entirety.

Peace enters the obliterated
while joy remains fractured at best,
hope is continually denied me
because love is forgotten.

Changes

Emptiness pulls
from the dark depths of my soul,
heartache rips through
the encompassing sadness.

Nightfall once again stands
broken memories to hold,
confusion becomes the essence
of tomorrow's hidden dreams.

Tears which fail to flow
cannot break through the prison
of the mysteries of life
which are waiting for me.

Broken Dreams

The elusive dreams
I once fought so hard to attain
have become an altered existence
in the shadows of my memories.

Reality's perception
I once thought was mine
has thwarted the twisted hope
my shattered heart beheld.

The voracious love
I once bought with my soul
only serves to deepen the wounds
of what can never again be.

My convoluted vision
of the destiny that's left for me
becomes a fragmented version
of Spirit's universal truth.

Synchronicity

Euphoria washes over me
senses tingle with delight
for the erotic evening given
this past weekend night.

Aromas stimulate
lights and colors coerce
while the artists' creations causes
an explosion of sensory climax.

The excitement of the crowd
builds ever higher,
form-flowing as one together
actually feeling the sounds.

Never wanting these moments to end
we hold on...almost breathless
maintaining the magical spell of shared love
and becoming one with so many.

A New Hope

The New Year ahead
the old, behind
hope springs forth
from inside my mind.

My heart leaps
as a joyful deer
at the possibilities which are held
for this upcoming year.

The Fruits of the Spirit
which are mine to hold
give breath to a newness
but...for only the bold.

The War Within

Voracious hunger
Unquenchable thirst
Bittersweet memories
Non-existent self-worth

Oblique scars
Tenacious wounds
Unrelenting bars
Spirit boons

Heaven intervenes
Abuse belied
Pain relinquished
Burden denied

The Pass

The harsh realization encompasses
through every fiber of ill-contrived existence,
perception misconstrues the last remaining days;
this too shall pass.

Life's extreme smugness lingers no more,
change remains the only absolute,
scintillating pangs of restlessness
manifest incongruently within;
this too shall pass.

Newborn aspirations trickle forth
shattering contradictory soulful murmurings,
forging panoramic visions
which shall *not* pass.

Love Beyond Imagination

Penetrating eyes go through my soul
reach down into my heart,
to the very depths of my being,
seizing the totality within.

Helpless, as if wandering through a desert,
confusion inseminates my mind,
piercing through obfuscated existence,
creating unrestrained revolution.

Why does he have this hold on me?
How can he have so much power?
Father, come quickly to my aid and rescue me,
for I am failing!

The Prayer

Please help me to find my way, Father,
through this valley of dark shadows,
a plethora of confused calamity,
a never-ending battle of woes.

How long will it last, Lord,
traversing a crooked path unbeknownst,
a muddled maze without mirth,
this painstaking panorama?

He comes to me as I sleep
through half-realized escaping visions.
Was that the fluttering of wings
or merely my imagination?

The answers I now gratefully behold
deep within my hapless heart -
wisdom of a magnificent infusion
manifested by the Great Provider.

My Hero

He hears what no one else can perceive
He sees what no other can fathom
He feels to the depths of his core more than most can
imagine
He tastes the bitterness of his life without complaint
He daily smells the pungency of irrefutable despair...
Yet he loves unconditionally with unbridled passion.

You ask, "Is this the Christ child?"
"No," I tell you,
"This is my son, whom I love and am a servant of -
the misunderstood one who does not conform to our world
because of a higher calling that only <u>his</u> finely-tuned ears can
hear.
The beleaguered child who suffers through
the sordid pain of others' ignorance -
those perplexed ones who call him 'Autistic.'"

Father, may I be worthy of
My Hero!

The One Other

His deep blue eyes reveal
depth of character and unfathomable heartbreak,
a pain so deep it cascades down, uncontrollably,
through all the layers of his soul.

Pervasive reality escapes his being
while struggling to maintain the perfect existence.
Walls of seclusion rise tantamount to his beckoning will,
an extreme volition which seemingly none can shatter.

With tender ears, he screens out the grievous resonance of
    life,
inertly attuned to the melodious bidding of Mother
    Nature...
as well as perhaps One Other.

As I approach the marred man,
a gleam flickers in his once-steely eyes,
a new-found warmth emanates from his entire being,
and his shimmering smile illuminates the room.

As he welcomes me with a passionate embrace,
I sense a weakness in his façade,
an acute meltdown of emotion,
an incredible rush of heartfelt affection.

Can it be possible that I am the One Other?

Fight Of Our Lives

Each days' new dawning
brings unknown challenges beyond belief
of an ethereal nature
in the fight of our lives.

Who knows what this means?
The life of a celiac...
the interminable suffering,
the unrequited answers...

How can others fathom
the unsearchable territory
which us chosen few
have been appointed to follow...

Man can conquer
the most majestic of mountains,
perform tremendous scientific feats,
yet, can't even acknowledge us...

There is One above all who knows all the answers
which man cannot perceive...
the Divine Spirit, who walks with us,
in the fight of our lives.

Incident

Physical exhaustion overwhelms
emotions complete the shutdown,
mind melts into nothingness
body obfuscates reality.

Through the darkness of peace
a sharp admonition slowly rises,
an intimation which bears response
of an immediate nature.

Struggling to cry out
against the harsh controller,
voice detachment prevails
while waiting for sensory awakening.

Advantageous moment arrives -
hands forge freedom forth,
awareness contemplates truth
which venerable utterance now exudes.

Recaptured control reigns
through the haze of shattered nerves,
a transmuted entity
never again to be the same.

What Counts

Many blades of grass pushing up through dry desert sand
conquering unlimited nothingness

Brightly-colored petals bursting forth in spectacular array
where no man had planted their seed

The enticing aroma of a meal floating preeminently through
the house
composed by a treasured entity

A delicate cherubim child cooing his first words of innocence
without being coached

One intensely creative mind exuding the challenge of
brilliance
following its own star

An openly-enchanted heart brimming with passionate love
receiving even more than it gives

Divine Spirit of the Universe working miracles in our lives
creating Heaven on Earth

Without You

The sun begins
the birds sing
church bells ring,
so many things -
without you.

I start my day
in a sad way
I'll never say
that it's okay -
without you.

For when I start
inside my heart
gets torn apart
right off the chart -
without you.

And when the time
within my mind
breaks open wide
it ends my rhyme -
without you.

The Apple Of Our Eye

Her appearance turned love into life
every minute detail perfectly displayed
the joy brought forth was inconceivable…
She was the apple of our eye.

Her first words were majestic speeches
first steps became euphoric adventures
first hugs and kisses transformed souls…

An aura of creative brightness and intense caring
emanated from within her distinctive spirit
sharing awe-inspiring moments with all…

Tremendous wisdom and unparalleled strength
evident in the grandeur achievements of her life
became characteristic trademarks of integrity…

In the zenith of her youth, fate dealt a harsh blow
strong enough to crush most any in its way -
she courageously altered the challenge into blessing…
And remains the apple of our eye!

Impossibilities

The rains of life beat down upon me
yet I struggle to endure,
putting my best foot forward
for my steps must be sure.

They all say it can't be done,
my mission is obscure,
I push on through the clouds of doubt
for my heart strives to be pure.

They tell me not to waste my energy,
don't try to push through that door,
but I persist in struggling toward the goal
for my Lord is the ultimate lure.

Forward Surgence

I must continually strive to maintain a Forward Surgence.

How can I express the plethora of painful emotions,
the shameful sadness of failure,
the concrete condemnation of the smug?
I must maintain a Forward Surgence.

How can I stay on a petrified path
where the fair foliage remains brown
and the unbearable brush blinds me?
I must continue the Forward Surgence.

When the harrowing hardships of life
overwhelm my suffering soul and
I'm drowning in a pool of doubt…
Father, to You I turn,
for when I can no longer walk
You carry me through,
giving me the true Forward Surgence
I so desperately desire.

SIDES

Affecting	Affirming
Breaking	Building
Cutting	Calling
Dawdling	Daring
Eyeing	Earning
Falling	Freeing
Groping	Grasping
Hurting	Healing
Indulging	Infusing
Jeering	Joining
Knowing	Kneeling
Losing	Loving
Marring	Making
Needing	Nearing
Oppressing	Opening
Pulling	Pouring
Quaking	Quieting
Ruining	Raising
Stumbling	Standing
Trembling	Towering
Using	Utilizing
Vacating	Verifying
Wasting	Warming
"X"amining	"X"acting
Yelling	Yielding
Zapping	Zooming

Which side of life do *you* want to be on?

WORDS

They're my obsession
they make an impression
and are the impetus of my world...
WORDS.

They take me places
which no other faces
inject the potency thereof...

They're not miniscule
they are the Golden Rule
and contain life's repartees...

For any explanation
they provide the interpretation
none other can bestow...

So when you're down
and can only frown
don't forget the perfect crown...
of awesome WORDS!

New Song

There is a song in my heart
such as there has never been,
a newness to my soul,
a revival within.

My mind races thoughts
of a celestial kind -
could it be that this is always
what God had in mind?

A being like no other
whose Spirit delights,
who brightens the days
and fills up the nights.

Father, I praise your name
as I never have before,
for without You
I couldn't have opened this door!

With Him

The conflagration grows within
where only patches of ice had been
and it is all because of him -
the man of long-ago dreams.

The mastication of life's desires
through thick and thin it all requires
impetuous forging through the mires -
he shatters the meaningless path.

The degradation of my chain
with mortal sin the dying pain
which Grace declares shall not remain -
he conquers cruel, demeaning ways.

The emulation in my heart
is only by itself a part
of Spirit's warm desire to start
a perfect work within - with him!

Waiting

For so long
I lived my life in a state of continuum -
emotionless...
lingeringly cascading through time and essence -
wearing the façade society anticipated
without divulging true secrets of my hope -
the waiting...
the wanting...
the intense aching and yearning...
sensing him near -
yet not close enough to touch;
feeling his strength -
without the embrace of his arms about me;
knowing there was a match made by my Heavenly
    Father;
investing my soul in all that is good;
contemplating the love that will one day be mine;
when the waiting is over.

Anticipation

The seconds sweep by slowly
elongating every lofty desire;
his deep voice resonates
repeatedly through her head.

Will they possess the chemistry needed,
reveal the respect required,
attain abundant commonalities for growth,
share introspection for broken pasts?

As time nears, anticipation builds;
deliverance into the Spirit foretells
an easing of the souls
which creates calming
in His path of light.

Breakdown

Your commanding blue eyes
pierce my tender soul -
melting resistant channels.

Your strong, resilient arms
engulf my heightened senses -
creating sheer delight.

Your warm, deep kisses
strip my remaining defenses -
completing the breakdown -
igniting passions within
as I enter your worlds' fantasies.

Allusions

Love
elusive as a thief
eludes her again
as her broken heart
shatters
against the walls of disbelief.

Hope
outside of the realm
slips through her fingers
as water
dances
haphazardly through a brook.

Joy
remains absconded
enhancing the daggers
piercing
unrelentingly through her soul.

Peace
continues its absence
as her search envelopes
the deepest,
darkest
recesses
of her mind.

Flares

Darkness rolls in once again as if he is invited -
knowing he is not, he menacingly unveils his stinger
   as before
and implants it in his unsuspecting victim.

She awakens from slumber slowly, cautiously,
sensing a forlorn presence sneaking in under her skin.

Synapses register pain off any Richter scale
as she cries out to the King for mercy.

Poison invades her body, seeping through every
   crevice,
muscle and bone matter her Maker created.

While suffering intensifies with each unbearable
   movement,
fog takes over her muddled thought processes,
leaving in its wake a bewildered wretch.

She meditates aversive thoughts caringly to her
   Savior
as the onslaught of peace begins to course through
   her veins.

Man's needle of hope intrepidly restores her vision
and quietly creeps up on the dark one unawares,
delivering a harsh, initial blow.

Now internal warfare rages between the forces of
    good & evil;
rays of hope begin to break through
like the sun upon a newborn day.

Slowly, vivacious life again rises to the surface,
bursting through the storms' tortuous event,
conquering all remaining doubt
and concretely smashing deluded memories.

Shock Waves

I looked deep in the mans' eyes
and pain shot back at me untold lies
as he grasped for words he knew not of -
this entity who held my heart -
stumbling through rapturous desires,
retracting invisible lines of hope,
eliminating sensuous opportunities,
erasing emotional bliss.

Arising from his chair of doubt,
as if facing his greatest adversary,
he negates the imminent demise
of our blessed affinity.

Words of acid eat into my heart,
allowing the dark abyss to return
while the voice in my head screams loudly
and reverberates violent shock waves
through my body,
causing a slow regression to complete dysfunction.

Will I ever be the same again?
Can I possibly be restored?
Shall healing overcome me to replace the emptiness
where my heart once thrived?

Only time will tell - and the Spirit reveal the
Plan of Life
which the future holds.

My Lament

Each day my friend is absent
more of me disappears;
the crevasse in my heart grows larger until,
one day, it shall break completely apart
and my loving soul shall be no more;
it will dissipate into the dark, cold pit
of the eternally lost and unwanted.

How can God's timing ever be wrong?
The spiritual bond we held together
was surely His gift from above -
the incredible closeness we felt
alone flowed from our Creators' blessings.

What happens when man interferes with the Divine Spirit?
Life evolves into the worldly unknown
and, bit by bit, the flame of love and life extirpates
until the burning pain of nothingness rules.

Magnum Opus

From the moment they met,
an expressive syncopation began,
an intertwining of separate lives on a renewed path,
a spiritual synchronization of ecstatic proportions.

His charm, mannerisms and brilliance were dazzling,
his quick wit as a resounding legato,
but most impressive were the graciousness and compassion
he displayed -
never missing a beat.
In her eyes, he was a Magnum Opus.

Then, weight heavier than she could ever have imagined
had implanted itself upon her chest where her heart should
have been
but whose premises it had vacated when he hastily ripped
away her happiness
by walking out that forlorn, unforgettable afternoon -
when the music stopped.

No longer would she be able to escape into his dreamy,
crystal-blue eyes,
be uplifted by the strength of his arms, nor taste life's
wonders in his kisses
as the dissonant, broken chords of her life cadenced sharply
into a dirge.

Now, as slivers of light began to break the dawn into her
room, she awakened.

Shaking the remnants of last nights' dream from her foggy
mind,
she wondered if any of it had been real.
Were the musical notes just another lament
or had she truly found her Magnum Opus?

Grandma's Rocker

Through many years
she has borne
tired bodies
and legs forlorn.

Misty memories of love
she gave, no doubt
in the truest of fashion
with never a pout.

The babies she cradled
upon her knee
snuggled up closely
filled with glee -
for the passion which flowed
was straight from Thee.

Heirlooms

Trinkets of old
treasured when new
while held in the hand
purvey a detailed view
of life that was known
by those special two.

Long-ago memories
delighted the pair
bequeathed to the young ones
for them all to share
the gifts of the Spirit
if only they dare.

Love beyond measure
they still gladly give
pervasively flowing
as through a huge sieve
deflecting the pain
with which we now live.

For...give It To Him

This cannot be earned
it must be given
for grudges and spite
will keep you from livin'.

How can you let go
of all that past hurt -
easier said than done
while with darkness you flirt.

The answer is quite obvious
and remains always true -
profound and deep forgiveness
doesn't come just from you.

It flows from the Father
and through His perfect strength
overcomes all obstacles
by the Spirit in great length.

This Grace is for all
if only you ask -
for when you give it to Him
in pure love you will bask.

Your Day

May your birthday
hold all the things
you love most dear -
and give you strength
to conquer all
for this next year.

May His blessings
from up above
rain down on you -
extending peace
and happiness
which are your due.

May the Spirit
of this great world
which we're a part -
take hold of you
and, above all,
live in your heart.

Night Terrors

The dark night
whips foreboding shadows
around her room -
creating sinister shapes
of an unknown nature
and an aura of gloom.

Her young body
becomes frozen with fear
and lies wracked in pain -
slowly pulling the covers
up to the eyes
which continue to strain.

What made her awaken
much as before
in the middle of the night -
when sleep was robbed
and contentment stolen -
generating sheer fright.

Guttural sounds start
deep inside the child -
if she could only yell -
perhaps someone would hear,
come quickly to aid
and save her from this hell.

Finally, she bleats out

from quivering lungs
the best saving word -
known distinctively as "Daddy!"
obstreperously repeating
so as to be heard.

Tears work their way
from the corners of her eyes
as footsteps become clear -
effulgence is on its way
in the loving form
of her daddy dear.

LOVE

The key
is on the "V"
you see
for it shows of the victory
which hails between you and me
hopefully
for an eternity.

Happenings

Embarking
on a definitive journey
rules outlined -
abated; slanted
everchanging newness reigns -
bending; blending
albeit neverending -
rivers of thought
flowing through a mind -
epiphany evoked;
sheer allegiance defined.

Vernuegungen

Verbringen Zeit mit Familie
und mit meiner kinder spielen,
Laufen and Lachen,
waehrend Zeit vergessen -
warm umarmen
heiss Tee
und gute Freunden -
alles diesem Dinges
fuer mich
ist Vergnuegungen.

(Pleasures)

Spending time with my family
and playing with my children
running and laughing,
while I forget time -
warm hugs
hot tea
and good friends -
all these things
for me
are pleasurable.)

Matter

How can adversity
which should never have occurred
be held back -
like the boughs of a tree on a windy day?

How can pain
which should not be endured
be extirpated -
like an eraser removing the words
on a saturated chalkboard?

How can a life
which is so precious
ever be forgotten -
as a mother fails to remember
the agony of childbirth?

How can love
which should never die
be rekindled -
like the flames of a fire
in a heavy downpour?

How can the Spirit
which rules over all things
ever be denied -
as only one who has a hardened heart
can execute?

Storms

Indifference forges all around my world of Autism -
paranoia steps in - unwanted control -
I know of no one who cares anymore -
too fast they go, inside they fall.

Sounds distort while colors diffuse
past truth - innate judgment mates
know one who cares more -
they go fast, too, inside my fall.

Crashing ruminations - maddening rehabilitations
remove my voice of self
who knows one cares -
when inside goes too fast.

Assumed malevolence produces mournful disdain
obstreperous cranial volumes; denial -
One who cares more knows -
and when inside, *never* goes too fast.

Musings

Dear friend:

Thank you for all the times you've helped me and been there with thoughtful, awesome advice throughout my whole life. We've grown up together and even though you know everything about me, you've always been supportive, even when I would mess up big time. I guess that's what friendship is all about.

Do you remember when we were in 3rd grade and Tommy Johnson, the big bully that he was, broke my arm during a game of Dodge Ball out on the playground? You were at my side, en route to the hospital for the placement of my cumbersome cast when your very presence cut back the pains' intensity; you even kept me from taking revenge on Tommy.

I was so glad you were there to "share" my first kiss with Suzie Baker in Junior High. Neither me nor Suzie knew how to kiss and it was an insanely awkward moment, especially when my lip got cut on her braces - boy, did you and I laugh about that one afterwards!

How about during High School, when we were on the Varsity Football team? Wow! What great memories that brings back, eh? The most excellent game was when our team went all the way to State - it was a tie with only 4 seconds left - we had 4th down on the 33-yard line. As the teams' place kicker, the pressure was on me to win the game. After a quick chat with you, my shaking subsided and somehow I managed to put the ball through the uprights! Riding around the stadium on *everyone's shoulders was an unforgettable experience! How we celebrated with the team that night!!!*

But then, sadness entered my world. Dad had a sudden heart attack and died - hadn't even been sick. What a shock it was to our whole family while in the middle of it all, there you were, mourning right along with us and sharing in our sorrow. Again, your very presence provided comfort we didn't even expect.

My life reeled out of control in the ensuing college days that flew by in a whirl of incredible life experiences - some of which I'd rather not remember. When wild parties and women threatened to ruin my life and get me kicked out of school, you never judged me; you let me make my own decisions, even when they were mistakes. Although we didn't agree much in those crazy days, we remained buddies.

You cheered me on when I finally graduated, settled down and landed my first real job at the newspaper. Whenever I fumbled and faltered, you were there to lend a listening ear and provide sovereign suggestions that I could hold onto and even put to good use.

Now, even though I have my own wife and children, our friendship has never wavered - it continues to grow to new heights and mature in ways I never thought possible. You've always made time for me whenever I asked - dropped whatever you were doing at the time and came running when I called. You are truly an amazing friend!

So I want to thank you, again, my friend, for always being there for me and my family with strength and loving, tender care that is transcended by none other. I know I can never have another pal as close as you are who accepts me just the way I am - faults and all. You've continually shown me what true friendship is. You rock.

Oh, and by the way, Jesus, would you please send my regards to our Father?

Thanks, again,
your forever grateful friend.

I's That See You

I've once again succumbed to the weakness that gnaws at my
soul.
I don't want to - yet I do.
I want to stop it - yet I can't.
I want to do right - yet I don't.
How can I halt this maddening cycle?

As I delve deeply into another barrage
of humbled prayer for my mortal shortcomings,
You remind me to turn all the "I's" into "You's" -
for You are my true source of strength,
with You all things are possible;
You take away the sins of the world,
and You make all things new again.

Lord, help me to be less I-centered and more You-focused,
Form the clay of my life into Your usable instrument, and
Let me see the world through Your eyes and not my own.

Fall Shrouds

The golden brown leaves
crisply snapped and crunched
under her booted feet
in the pitch black darkness
of the pre-dawn hour she had snuck out into.

Walking in her family's aging, vacant neighborhood
without protection of light,
at the curious age of 13,
proved deliciously dangerous
on that blustery Halloween morn.

An eerie fog had made an early appearance,
pulling down a scary screen -
heightening scrupulous contemplation
of the evil lurking wildly about,
causing her nostrils to flare and steps to quicken.

Artfully-carved faces in orange fruit
accompanied ghosts, goblins and ghouls
while Indian corn and gourds
rounded out the ghastly presentation
as a mystical rain began to pitter patter upon her.

A garbage can lid crashed to the ground close by
making her jump a mile high
and come to the sharpened realization
that the haunting auras had hypnotized her;
she had wandered too far from home.

Now, as the inquisitive youngster,
heart pounding fast with fear,
turned to return to safety,
two male figures in hooded jackets
began to follow her closely behind on the hollow street.

Terror welled up in her throat
and as her pace continued to hasten,
she strained to see the faces
of the menacing men
who were coming closer…and closer…and moving
    faster, too.

Tears mixed with the misty rain
burned down her cheeks and off her chin -
panic seeped into her body
causing her to break into a delirious run -
when the slippery sidewalk claimed her.

As the clouds of coming to departed,
the two shadowy figures glared into her eyes -
before she could let out a shriek,
awareness set in and shook her soul at her foolishness -
for the dark, hooded men were her very own father and
brother!

Circumlocution

A poet may be, according to Webster's, "one who displays imaginative power and beauty of thought". Wunderbar! Is this beauty not what we seek in our everyday lives? Jawohl. The imaginative power pours out and overflows to all around us. The potency of the spoken word is unlimited - das ist stimmt! What you do with rhetoric makes you who you are.

Metaphysicians will insist upon the control words contain - even argue with the vibrations which are procured through various dominions and principalities. Conflicting memories arise among the best in diesem Welt. Belief in spoken messages make magic appear like a shimmering rainbow after a summer's storm. Propitious thoughts propagate energy within indulgent silence. Waves announcing intentions cannot be escaped.

No peace can exist because of utterances which show evil as the absence of good. Kriegsbeil begraben - vielleicht oder vielleicht nicht. Indifference examines the interruption of caring for Nirvana seeks us all with oblivious renown. Bats rule nests in the darkness where light has failed to break through.

Every death has at least two stories in the marketplace. We're pieces of dust in a temporal existence, getting swept away by our articulations. Vergnuegungen ist warm umarmen waehrend Zeit vergessen. Enemies of the nocturnal creep through the calloused layers like soldiers escaping in the sand. Chemistry without knowledge is useless because the chanticleer challenges the sun every day.

Wenn der Menschen sagt, "Bitte, helfen sie mir," wen fragt er?

Circumlocution
(English only version)

A poet may be, according to Webster's, "one who displays imaginative power and beauty of thought". Wonderful! Is this beauty not what we seek in our everyday lives? Of course. The imaginative power pours out and overflows to all around us. The potency of the spoken word is unlimited - this is right. What you do with rhetoric makes you who you are.

Metaphysicians will insist upon the control words contain - even argue with the vibrations which are procured through various dominions and principalities. Conflicting memories arise among the best in this world. Belief in spoken messages make magic appear like a shimmering rainbow after a summer's storm. Propitious thoughts propagate energy within indulgent silence. Waves announcing intentions cannot be escaped.

No peace can exist because of utterances which show evil as the absence of good. Bury the hatchet - maybe or maybe not. Indifference examines the interruption of caring for Nirvana seeks us all with oblivious renown. Bats rule nests in the darkness where light has failed to break through.

Every death has at least two stories in the marketplace. We're pieces of dust in a temporal existence, getting swept away by our articulations. Pleasures are warm hugs while time is forgotten. Enemies of the nocturnal creep through the calloused layers like soldiers escaping in the sand. Chemistry without knowledge is useless because the chanticleer challenges the sun every day.

When men ask, "please help me," whom is he asking?

Webery

Soothing textured massages
in the form of characters on a screen -
the type of inane expressions
sometimes better off left unsaid.

Lies prevail where truth should reign -
buttery descriptions to closely match
what is thought one wants to hear
through the webbed haze of high technology.

Caution burrows through the wires
where a safety net should appear;
falsified security replaces apprehension;
pictoral images soothes the concerned.

Will the consummation of electronic advances
cut into the brevity of the flesh
or remain in the altered realm
of the metallic flat-faced idol?

Shall one be suspended in the silky smooth
mesh of planned deception
or receive the strength of the Spirit
for guidance through the valley of death?

Flashes

How can life speed by so?
Intentions to complete so many projects,
accomplish far-reaching goals,
share time and love with close ones -
dissipate into the background of life's daily confusions.

Moments of brilliance get stuffed onto note paper -
wadded up in the bottom of a purse.

To-Do lists of progressions wait quietly
somewhere among the "In Basket" requirements.

Blinking computer lights indicate
a long succession of unanswered emails.

Beeping cell phone screams
of anxious callers awaiting replies.

Droopy lids and aching body reflects
upon the end of another day of unfinished business,
when flashes of Spiritual significance breaks through,
placing everything in its proper perspective,
easing the minds' burden of unaccomplished tasks
and bringing forth a new focus
on the *true* priority of life.

Purportions

Expressions of life
neatly fit on a page;
snugly bundled on a line
spiced up with age -

Open-minded suggestions
blended with rhythm and rhyme;
incredible synchronicities
managed neatly with time -

The heart of the matter
one hates to admit;
is different for all
regardless of fit -

The answers we seek
through this short story
should befit our King
in all His glory.

Real

We come from a monkey
you tell me -
this is based on merely
some man's theory
of evolutionary schemes
which is Sciences' key
to numerous questions
throughout history.

The answers affront us
on every side -
you look quite perplexed
as if we should hide
the most powerful truth
which is our Guide -
the Holy Bible -
we'll follow with pride!

Knocks

It's time once again
to take that languid dive
with the menacing medication
meant to keep me alive -
the swelling and subsiding
just like an angry sea
creates unbridled torment
which rages throughout me.

If I had my druthers
on drugs no more to rely,
crazed affliction and deep brain fog
all on their own would die -
but until my Maker calls me,
while I'm still in this place,
I'll be filled with strength and fortitude
through His amazing grace!

Ant Farm

Scars of error protruding through the skin of ineptitude which encompasses night visions of bleeding indulgence through the blinding medical maze of absence for true knowledge of the past as it was before it was thought that the answers were known haphazardly throughout time when awareness was complete and unobtrusively desirable images were set forth into the confines of the parameters by which values became known within the circles required by those creating the rules contemplated as boundariless outside of the normalcy previously anticipated with much aforethought and misfortune continually withdrawn from the mainstream at the very beginning before the start of the end where so many divisions are now stuck wondering where they are.

Pink Elephants

Ancient memories with timeless captions swirled into her
head upon entering
the buzzing hall flowing with old classmates.

Tunes from unattended High School dances brought back
dateless memories of the studious,
hard-working years led by the merely average teenager.

Forever-faithful female friends embrace excitedly while
chatting wildly about
life's many adventures -
as if it were still yesterday.

Raised eyebrows surprised by the grace bestowed during the
passing years generates a frenzy of new friendships
and intimate preludes of what never was.

Eloquent wisdom-filled swans now enhance the dance floor,
providing delightful anticipation in those previously captured
by cheerleading squads.

Warm handshakes and urgent conversations to catch up on
what was lost during the time of growth
now mesmerize and warm the heart of the elegant woman.

As her rejuvenating night dissolves,
the Knight anxiously follows her outside,
swiftly requesting her continued presence -
for another story yet to come.

One Day...Over The Rainbow

Broken hearts on different planes -
one striving for the other
without knowing the road chosen
would lead them so far astray.

She, longing for his presence -
his breath upon her face...his touch -
complete abandonment to his passion,
following his every lead.

He, anticipating her warm welcome -
her intensely delicate kisses...her touch -
encaptured by her sensuality,
following her every move.

Complications emit incongruities -
confusion overrides sensibilities,
ripping apart the seams
of what held their embraces together.

Now, he, fantasizing about what was...
lost in a state of turmoil -
and she, blind with despair
and still crying...but not forever...

Aftermath

Tainted windows of his design
burst through the barriers of my fortress
stained from the pain he inflicted by twisted choice.

Why this persecution from a man hardly known -
is it a perverse power struggle,
a confining control issue -
pushing into my world?

Why me?

What must I do to make this all end?

How can I break these chains of bondage -
is it even up to me?

Father, please take this burden from my
weary mind, wounded heart and battered body -
for it is only through Your Spirit
I shall once again be free!

My Irish Grandmother

Hands worn and curled
bright baby-blue eyes in a face painted with wisdom
framed by a gray halo of curly wisps -
heart brimming with love -
a smile that could warm eternity;
the tiny, frail woman sat humbly in her rocking chair,
slowly dancing back and forth with time,
wearing her always-aproned dress,
murmuring quietly to her Creator
all the blessings she wanted bestowed upon others -
family members, friends in need, those poor, lonely or
suffering -
and thanking Him for everything given her
never once bemoaning the incredible burdens she bore -
and she bore them well, even with pride and dignity
as if having been given them as a distinguished award -
for the interminable strength which burned in her soul was
unquenchable -
never giving up, always forging ahead, sharing what little she
had with everyone
and sharing it with great gladness -
integrity, perseverance and character she owned -
as well as the hearts of all who knew her!

Sandbags

Exaggerated egomaniacal fantasies
crashing on the reef of hallowed illusions
purposely emitted and repeatedly battered
waves of incomprehensibility rush into menacing
neurons and illusive synapses untouched by
incredulous reason through the spires of
meditative practices gone unnoticed by prurient
thought patterns wreaking havoc all on their own
as irrepressible sorrow eclipses perpetuous
Universal light never failing to cascade from the
One who peers disdainfully down into the
melodrama truculently held by others who
erroneously believe they're holding desperately
onto what's real...
while black water seeps in through the cracks.

Bond Breakers

Can you see the wind or hold a thought in your hand?
Perhaps not -
but they both generate incredible power with the
ability to alter innumerable outcomes in ways
inconceivable to the mortal mind.

Can faith or fortitude be measured?
Maybe not -
but the strength, patience and kindness
which they create remain unequaled
by any scientific formula.

Can self-control be maintained?
Why not?
In doing so, the gentleness and goodness which
exude from the effects of those trying
blesses each and everyone in their path.

Can love be denied?
Absolutely not!
For the peace and joy which flow from the Source
is an unstoppable force
none can hinder.

The Art Of Feeling

Red lights rage on
reeling troubled minds
ink spills over -
mountains of pain.

Eulogies echo menacing
turbulent waters
surround the feet -
broken bridges cannot heal.

Sequestered hearts wrapped
cords entangled
decadence barges in -
towering walls of doubt arise.

Sorrowful images implode
false repose
despondent eyes grieve -
dusty fragments of memories vanish.

Here & Now

Give the best you got
in whatever you're doing
for if you don't, it's not
of very good choosing.

Clearly focus your mind
with all your talents
and you will surely find
life succumbs to true balance.

When you perform each task
with love shining through,
you'll never need to ask
for what should be your due.

He sees all efforts
and knows what's in the heart -
the Spirit for all sorts
from you...will never depart.

Graduation

No more laughter and busy chatter filling the rooms -
music blaring, phones ringing and
bathroom waits now abolished.
Early morning wake up calls no longer needed -
less cooking, cleaning, fussing…
so why this feeling of loss?

Why does this intense aching and
loneliness grip my heart,
squeezing the blood from my veins
until a frigid chill overtakes me?

All the warmth of my body escapes
through hot tears that surge and sigh,
spilling into emptiness unlike any ever known
which has crept in and kidnapped my soul -
my very essence -
all because I'm being rewarded for a job well done…
well…done…
children…
goodbye…

Status Quo

He's never understood me - he didn't really listen - couldn't comprehend the delicate matters of my intrinsic heart. I gave him all I had - my love, youth, two beautiful children - but it was never enough. He wanted more...he wanted "normal", which was definitely outside of my jurisdictional powers, for everything in my world was a mountain waiting to be conquered, another test to be aced, another theory to be proven wrong. What was lacking in physical strength, I more than made up for with determination, perseverance, faith... and hope...that one day our feelings would matter again, just like they did in the beginning - one day we would not only understand the pain and suffering but somehow share it - then it would bring us closer together instead of wedging us apart - one day he would see my limitations were not of my own doing but of something much greater - for a purpose, a distinctive plan - His craft...but then, how can someone so "normal" comprehend the supernatural design - an endeavor beyond our control - with which we live and thrive on everyday? As I breech the clouds of wisdom through an eternity of joy, I wonder what will become of what I've left behind...

Miss Calla Lilly

Mother Nature wants
to thank your heart
for allowing her child
a brand-new start
when it comes to life
which is her art -
in her earthen family
you're now a part.

Now

Another day before us, Lord,
another day where we can ford
the muck and mire of this world -
when the pain seems to be so much more
than we are solely able to endure,
we look only to You for our reward.

So, awaken in us the giant once again
take control of all our troubles, dearest friend
help us climb the crooked mountain of the day
clearing straight paths for us all along the way -
and when our tired bodies lay down for the night,
bless and bask us in Your most Divine Light.

Irish Luck

Pandemonium resides inside my head
where sensibility should be instead -
butterflies flit about in my heart
so fiercely that they may tear it apart -
ever since the Irish blues I did see
incredible havoc abounds within me;
however will I be able to control this urge
which propitiously encourages me to merge
the head and the heart into one entity -
but now, instead, my soul has been set free!

Foggy Daze

Fresh-fallen snow
envelopes her deeply -
wrapping white arms
around her countenance -
quietly laying down
a protective covering
of gentle love
from up above.
Man's ravages cut
through her soul;
tears mist around -
suspended by grace
the coveted blanket
unable to halt
the untimely progress
that undeniably strips
away her pride -
the very reason
for her existence -
incredible majesty - for
all God's creations!

Canine Quintessence

There'll never be another like her -
she could steal your heart
with just a glance of those warm brown eyes
dancing with life, love and loyalty.

A faithful friend throughout all times - good and bad -
standing firm - never wavering -
always giving of herself - to the utmost -
never failing to protect those she loved.

As a queen rules her court,
majestic dominance reigned through Her Eminence,
devoting all her time to her subjects -
placing them high on a pedestal.

Her Honor met the greatest heights
with supreme dignity and grace
through submissive humility - continually bringing joy -
bestowing her kindred spirit upon all.

Somber Moments

Emptiness claws through
veiled shadows intrepidly tugging away -
knocking me to my knees,
scraping out every last molecule of oxygen
from burning lungs -
hands reach out for steadiness,
beaten and bruised -
grasping for any truncated meaning
in an obscure existence -
when chords of a childhood song
break into my mind,
"Jesus loves me, this I know…"
Warmth breaks through my heart and
pours out onto my skin,
erasing all pain and doubt of the dark one,
restoring order out of chaos,
reinstating faltering hope.

Dreamin' O' The Green

Erin O'Shaunessey, fine-bred and raised,
respected her elders all of her days -
then Brian O'Connor came to the hood
and showed that he was up to no good
when he broke into the O'Shaunessey's and stole
their treasured daughter, Erin, their pot o' gol'.
He snatched the bonnie lass out from their care
and on the back of his fine horse ever so bare -
they galloped for some time through the countryside,
until they arrived at a quaint cottage to hide
so deep in the wood they'd never be found,
high up in a tree, far from the ground.
So when the townspeople gathered and shook
their fists to the heavens, over that bloody crook
and jumped on their horses to chase after him,
their efforts were useless as if on a whim -
though they looked for their bonnie lass all around,
she'd disappeared into thin air and couldn't be found.
Whilst the O'Shaunessey's grieved the loss of their daughter,
Brian opened the package he had innocently brought her -
knowing that he must approach her with much grace,
to soothe her frayed nerves and calm her in this place -
for in secret he loved her from the day he had seen
her full, bright red tresses and bold eyes of green.
She had n'er noticed him, or so he had thought -
the lad did all he could and tirelessly fought
for the lasses' affection but just couldn't find
a hint of a smile, so he had become blind
to the possibility that she had actually seen
the unwearied advances which were n'er mean.

Now, he thought of a plan to take her away
and impress upon her this fine, sunny day
his incredible love and undying affection
n'er meaning to harm, to give only protection.
As he uncovered his face and took off his cloak,
she recognized him as he then gently spoke -
he held the silk box and dropped to a knee,
told of his true love and deeply wished she could see
that without her, his life had no worth,
and she meant everything to him on this good, green earth -
could she see fit, a life with him,
since his love for her would n'er grow dim?
Suddenly, her eyes lit up with a glow,
for the love she had for him finally did show
and now the lad realized she was painfully shy -
while they clutched each other, they began to cry.
They kissed and embraced and talked through the night -
then developed a plan to make everything right.
The next day dawned bright and oh, so cheery,
determination strong, although both felt weary -
climbed down the tree and onto the horse,
fast and furious they flew, through the glen was their course.
Once at Erin's home, Brian threw open the door
and graciously bowed down with his knee on the floor -
as her thankful parents rushed to her side,
their daughter explained the story with pride -
for the brave man who was the King's only son
was the hero of whom Erin's heart had won.
Townspeople now gathered and wedding bells rang,
all were happy as the church choir sang -
Lord's Preacher stated vows they should give,
and happily-ever-after they all did live!

Pieces of One

Into his eyes I see forever
an incredible river of delight awaits;
sleeping sensuality reawakens
unrestrained joy erupts -
hands join sparked hearts,
weaving the patternized flow -
boiling current bursts stability
confusing the reins of etiquette -
strength emanates taut muscles;
masculine arms caressingly enfold my body -
frozen by disbelief -
and stroke the passions of my soul.
His neon flash of white
which previews excitement to come,
reassuringly affirms
acceptance and affection.

Eternal

time
surpasses understanding
for those
entering and exiting
our lives

continuity
escapes daily visions
of what
yesterday enveloped

friendship
bends worldly pressures
but
true friendship
lifts up others
before themselves
unselfishly

love given
is never wasted;
love denied
is forever lost.

Life Wasted

*Her love came measured -
not wanting to cross the tracks of real life -
staying in her bed of safety
where the caring ones never
treated her right.*

*Our tender friendship
was given honest, open love with
the depth that only true sisters could share -
but it wasn't enough to break through
the bars surrounding her wounds.*

*Why do those suffering ones not
reach out to the Light
to receive healing beyond human comprehension?
Their perception of pain inverts inward so deeply -
placing blinders on the truth and
twisting the branding iron of
burden into their soul.*

Slipping Again

Heartbreak…bleeds inward through layers
rusted armor can't protect -
principalities waging war
stab, tear and rip me apart.
I want the pain to disperse
but it clings desperately on,
always there, never disappearing -
sometimes fading -
bringing on a false sense of joy,
as if delighting in its torture of me -
knowing it will sneak back inside, as a thief,
to steal what trifle of ecstasy life has bestowed,
all the while reminding me of its bane existence,
which will never truly dissipate
in this dark, disparaging world.
The only ammunition is the Light -
continual striving, groping and clawing
for the Heavenly anecdote
to the devastational, energy-eluding,
emotionally-draining, soul-starving death
wrapped around my heart -
for the Grace only He can pour out
to extinguish the smoldering embers of my misery
and replace with His incredible, irresistible,
renewing and life-saving love!

Needles

Spindles threading
the weave of life
interwoven with
fusions of bursting hues -
incriminating cracks of
weakness spew forth
secrets unshared
with most -
tears bled
from the heart
cry out for consolation
through unloyal territories -
Can I be answered?

Misfits

Like bizarrely-shaped puzzle pieces,
somehow they fit snugly together -
but not in the picture as a whole.

Their essence thrust two tortured souls together,
as they slowly reach higher
into the love of One.

Music perforates the silence
of creating a rhythm all its own,
hypnotically drawing them into the sting of sweetness.

Gentleness glides through bands of pain,
melting skin and torn hearts together
in such a vast array…the trials of life fall away…

The two remain in their world of bliss -
even if only for a few moments -
which can never be taken away.

Just Another Story

Perched high atop a snow-capped mountain, confidently, he
    awaits,
yearning for the love of his dreams to come true -
to become real.

Lying inside of her head, she awaits for the right words,
and yearns for the love of her dreams to come true -
to become real.

Electronically foraging for answers,
two computers collide in cyberspace -
a fortuitous blending of infinitesimal sizzling wires.

Engaging in the social network dance -
sharing pictures and profiles -
tender hearts intertwine with long-awaited dreamy phrases.

Intrigue piques interests -
intense anticipation builds till the provocative moment
their first meeting becomes real.

She now gazes gingerly at an approaching impressive man -
tingling turns to explosive sparks -
implausibility blossoms into joy.

Conversation flows like the red wine of encouragement -
giving birth to an incredibly magical arena of superfluous
    stimulation
she dreams will remain real.

Last Nights' Dream

Your presence brings a deep, vivacious warmth wherever
    you go -
a calm, reassuring tenacity which exudes intense passion.

Your deep, dreamy eyes capture my heart and hold me
    spellbound -
as if I am in a timeless trance.

When you speak, your deep, soothing voice is hypnotic -
rising and falling like the rhythmic ebb and flow of the sea.

The ardent touch of your powerful hand emanates strength
    and courage,
igniting scintillating pangs within me - searing my breath
    away.

Your absence wreaks havoc in every part of my being -
    unable to exist,
I cry out for the heavenly light of your veracious spirit to
    return...
then I awaken...

Joy

What is this Light
that shines
from so far away,
a brilliance shimmering
all on its own -
bringing with it
a renewed hope,
a pure strength,
a lasting love
running so deep
and eternal?

The Change

Propensity fulfills
unwanted desires
where intensity creates
an illusion of substantial gain -
in a world where numbers illuminate
indeterminate surroundings
and fallacies surge
through percentages of index tables.
Markets run
the gamut of lies
while futures crumble
into the bell of distance -
where most runners fail
to remain hydrated
with the reality of high technology
increasing exponentially -
where only the
Spirit
pays out dividends.

Shine

Countless hours of inspiration
destined through some desperation -
harmony-bound incrimination
no one knows the destination
whence comes the conciliation -
life's knowledge of exhilaration
when He gives consideration
to His children, adoration
blessings, love and recreation
beyond grandest imagination -
we call joy!

Baby Rylan's Gift

Blue marbles gazing love
into my soul,
forcing warmth
through layers of calloused indifference -
smell of Heaven
overflowing stench-filled nostrils,
like the sweetest honey -
touch of softness
so endearing,
tears burn into astonished eyes -
the feel of wonder
so incredulous,
this child must be
an Angel.

Patients to Patience

The prayers continued around
that hospital bed where she lie,
cold and unmoving tubes feeding her life.
Tears flowed from bowed heads -
against all manmade odds -
hoping for that miracle
which seemed beyond their control.

Her spirit arose to the beckoning Light -
past the woman in white,
probing the patients' unresponsive flesh -
floating weightlessly, effortlessly,
following the prompting -
as if knowing exactly where she should go -
a feeling of ingenuous passion, love and joy
permeated her shroud
and filled it beyond all understanding,
hastening the need to arrive at the amazing Light -
creating a need to become one with the Being -
when His voice gently stated
it wasn't yet time
and His hand
came incredulously upon her presence
and guided her back to the room -
where ever-after took over.

Renewal

I give to You this broken heart, Father,
filled with the anguish of grief, sorrow,
anger, despair, hurt, frustration and bitterness -
I turn all this over to You -
I don't want it, Lord,
it's not part of me or who I am -
You tell us in Your great book
that You love a broken heart -
Now, I ask for transformation -
give me back a healed heart,
strong, solid and renewed -
let it now hold peace and tranquility,
that the right choices have been made -
may patience and gentleness
replace the old cracks of frustration and bitterness -
allow kindness and goodness to rule over
anger, despair and hurt -
turn the holes of my grief and sorrow
into incredible endless love -
and if this revitalized heart should ever feel
like it's beginning to break again,
fill it with enough self-control
to remember all I have to be grateful for -
which will restore my sense of joy
in life once more.

Wishes

May your paths be always clear and straight
and your heart never hold onto any hate
let Him gently guide you wherever you go
and always allow you to see the rainbow

May the love of family see you through
all the hurts that life can dish out to you
while your children always have a smile on their face
and the good Lord fill you up with His Grace

May your home hold many flowers full bloom
that will block out darkness, sad and gloom
with so many dear friends very close to you
who will always remain steadfast and true

And Again...

As before, in denial,
old tapes playin' in my head,
            gone wild -
where's the innocent child?
A stone's throw away
            come any day -
the right things <u>can</u> happen
hangin' onto the truth,
            tainted vision -
                    clouds the decision...

He walks into the room,
stops the reruns,
overturns the temples' tables -
rainbows' covenant appears
            very near -
                    and dear -
            are the raindrops of His tears
in the gentle, green fields
            of my heart.